WORKBOOK

AWAKENING

A DREAM JOURNAL

ELLEN FOREMAN, Ph.D.

A JANE LAHR ENTERPRISE

STEWART, TABORI & CHANG
NEW YORK

Design: Jeff Batzli
           J. C. Suarès
Consulting Photo Research: Natalie Goldstein

Reproduction credits
PAGES 4 TO 35: *Coffin of Khnumnakhte*, detail, ca.
1991–1786 B.C. Egyptian. The Metropolitan Museum
of Art, Rogers Fund, 1915.
PAGES 36 TO 67: *Ceremonial Robe*, detail, nine-
teenth or twentieth century, Native American
(Chilkat, Tlingit). The Metropolitan Museum of Art,
The Michael C. Rockefeller Memorial Collection,
Bequest of Nelson A. Rockefeller, 1979.
PAGES 6 8 TO 96: *Stela of 'Ofenmut*: detail of
*'Ofenmut Offering before Horus, Sun's Barque
above*, ca. 1991–1786 B.C., Egyptian. The Metropolitan Museum of Art, Museum Excavations,
1911–1912.

88 89 90 91 92 9 8 7 6 5 4 3 2 1

ISBN 1-55670-033-4

Published in 1988 by Stewart, Tabori & Chang, Inc.,
740 Broadway, New York, New York 10003.
Distributed by Workman Publishing, 708 Broadway,
New York, New York 10003.

Printed in Japan.

Keeping Track of Your Dreams

Just as people keep journals and appointment diaries to document the events of their waking lives, the dream journal lets you keep an ongoing record of the developments and changes in your inner life. This workbook has been designed especially for recording dreams. Its wide margins offer ample space for illustrations, questions, and afterthoughts.

Remember:

~~ Keep this workbook by your bedside every night and record, either during the night or in the morning, your nightly dream adventures.

~~ Carefully date your dreams. Chronology may not seem to matter now, but it will play a larger role in your future dream work.

~~ Do not worry about keeping within the lines if you write in the dark. *What* you write is far more important than neatness.

~~ Whenever possible, record the significant events of the day before and note what you have on schedule for the next day so you have a permanent record to refer to as you search for the meaning of your dreams. Some connections between real events and dreaming ones will not occur to you until later.

~~ If you cannot describe an image or scene in words, sketch it in the margin.

Soon you will understand the language of your dreams and your dreams will speak to you.

DATE: 6/17

TIME: _____

DATE:_____

TIME:_____

DATE:_____

TIME:_____

DATE: _____

TIME: _____

DATE:_____

TIME:_____

DATE:_____

TIME:_____

DATE:_____

TIME:_____

DATE:_____

TIME:_____

DATE:_____

TIME:_____

DATE:_____

TIME:_____

DATE:_____

TIME:_____

DATE:_____

TIME:_____

DATE:_____

TIME:_____

DATE:_____

TIME:_____

DATE:_____

TIME:_____

DATE:_____

TIME:_____

DATE:_____

TIME:_____

DATE:_____

TIME:_____

DATE:_____

TIME:_____

DATE:_____

TIME:_____

DATE:_____

TIME:_____

DATE:_____

TIME:_____

DATE:_____

TIME:_____

DATE:_____

TIME:_____

DATE:_____

TIME:_____

DATE:_____

TIME:_____

DATE:_____

TIME:_____

DATE:_____

TIME:_____

DATE:_____

TIME:_____

DATE:_____

TIME:_____

DATE:_____

TIME:_____

DATE:_____

TIME:_____

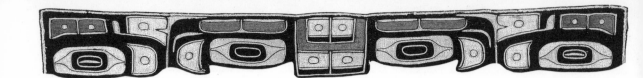

DATE:_____

TIME:_____

DATE:_____

TIME:_____

DATE:_____

TIME:_____

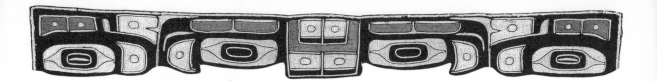

DATE:_____

TIME:_____

DATE:_____

TIME:_____

DATE:_____

TIME:_____

DATE:_____

TIME:_____

DATE:_____

TIME:_____

DATE:_____

TIME:_____

DATE:_____

TIME:_____

DATE:_____

TIME:_____

DATE:_____

TIME:_____

DATE:_____

TIME:_____

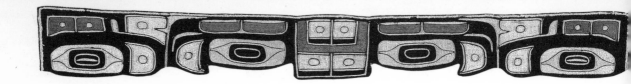

DATE:_____

TIME:_____

DATE:_____

TIME:_____

DATE:_____

TIME:_____

_____
_____
_____
_____
_____
_____
_____
_____
_____
_____
_____
_____
_____
_____
_____
_____
_____
_____
_____
_____
_____
_____

DATE:_____

TIME:_____

_____

_____

_____

_____

_____

_____

_____

_____

_____

_____

_____

_____

_____

_____

_____

_____

_____

_____

_____

_____

_____

DATE:_____

TIME:_____

DATE:_____

TIME:_____

DATE:_____

TIME:_____

DATE:_____

TIME:_____

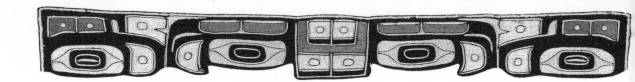

DATE:_____

TIME:_____

_____
_____
_____
_____
_____
_____
_____
_____
_____
_____
_____
_____
_____
_____
_____
_____
_____
_____
_____
_____
_____
_____
_____

DATE:_____

TIME:_____

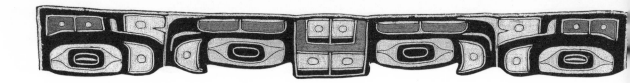

DATE:_____

TIME:_____

DATE:_____

TIME:_____

_____
_____
_____
_____
_____
_____
_____
_____
_____
_____
_____
_____
_____
_____
_____
_____
_____
_____
_____
_____
_____

DATE:_____

TIME:_____

DATE:_____

TIME:_____

DATE:_____

TIME:_____

_____
_____
_____
_____
_____
_____
_____
_____
_____
_____
_____
_____
_____
_____
_____
_____
_____
_____
_____
_____
_____
_____
_____
_____

DATE:_____

TIME:_____

_____
_____
_____
_____
_____
_____
_____
_____
_____
_____
_____
_____
_____
_____
_____
_____
_____
_____
_____
_____
_____
_____

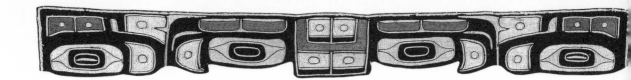

DATE:_____

TIME:_____

_____
_____
_____
_____
_____
_____
_____
_____
_____
_____
_____
_____
_____
_____
_____
_____
_____
_____
_____
_____
_____
_____
_____
_____

DATE:_____

TIME:_____

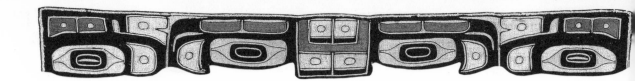

DATE:_____

TIME:_____

_____

_____

_____

_____

_____

_____

_____

_____

_____

_____

_____

_____

_____

_____

_____

_____

_____

_____

_____

_____

_____

_____

DATE: _____

TIME: _____

DATE:_____

TIME:_____

DATE:_____

TIME:_____

DATE:_____

TIME:_____

DATE:_____

TIME:_____

DATE:_____

TIME:_____

DATE:_____

TIME:_____

DATE:_____

TIME:_____

DATE:_____

TIME:_____

DATE:_____

TIME:_____

_____
_____
_____
_____
_____
_____
_____
_____
_____
_____
_____
_____
_____
_____
_____
_____
_____

 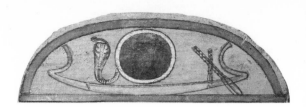

DATE:_____

TIME:_____

DATE:_____

TIME:_____

 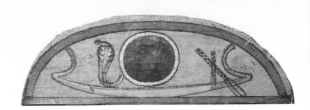

DATE:_____

TIME:_____

_____
_____
_____
_____
_____
_____
_____
_____
_____
_____
_____
_____
_____
_____
_____
_____
_____
_____
_____
_____
_____

DATE:_____

TIME:_____

DATE:_____

TIME:_____

DATE:_____

TIME:_____

DATE:_____

TIME:_____

DATE:_____

TIME:_____

DATE:_____

TIME:_____

DATE:_____

TIME:_____

 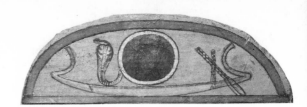

DATE:_____

TIME:_____

DATE:_____

TIME:_____

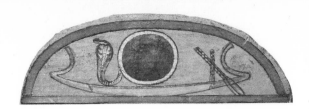

DATE:_____

TIME:_____

DATE:_____

TIME:_____

_____

_____

_____

_____

_____

_____

_____

_____

_____

_____

_____

_____

_____

_____

_____

_____

_____

_____

_____

_____

DATE:_____

TIME:_____

DATE:_____

TIME:_____

DATE:_____

TIME:_____

DATE:_____

TIME:_____

DATE:_____

TIME:_____